A Brain Composed of Stardust And Moon Rocks

Jillian Johnson

BookLeaf Publishing

Presentation by *BookLeaf Publishing*

Web: www.bookleafpub.com

E-mail: info@bookleafpub.com

ISBN: 9789357745086

First edition 2023

To my family, for helping me get to this point and always pushing me to be the best. Thank you for your unconditional love.

To my best friends, Isaac, Sky, Kat, and Jerrilyn, for being my biggest supporters, my fan club, and my true soul connections. I couldn't be here without your presence in my life, no matter how far apart life has taken us. I love you all, more than any string of words could ever portray.

Most importantly, I want to dedicate this book to the love of my life, and a true partner in crime, Mack. You have helped me navigate this crazy world, and I'd be truly misplaced without your guidance. My love for you is so grand, even the brutal force of nature is in awe, by the remarkable grace of it.

ACKNOWLEDGEMENT

To BookLeaf for helping me make the grueling process of publication easy!

 To J, who helped motivate and push all of these emotions to this page today. You the are my most revered love, and one of my greatest teachers. I will love you until the end of time. -J

PREFACE

This book will be full of fixation, agony, bliss, hatred, and every rapid feeling that washes over me, like the true chaos of ocean tide. As someone who deals with chronic overthinking and a brain that holds the secrets to the universe, these pages carry the words of my many worlds and forms. These works were carefully extracted from my soul, and splattered across the paper, for the moons to marvel at in astonishment. Not even moons know how far the universe stretches, even as they get lost in it.

-exile

You are too golden to go back where you've already been denied. If they didn't want to feel the warmth of your gaze, let them freeze to death in the cold of your indifference. Look down at the scars you keep from the frost that was once biting at your skin, while you begged for entry to the places that never understood your glory.

-Icarus died for a love he
could never comprehend

If I am the sun, then you are the menial Icarus
who could never touch me, as you simply do not
have the capacity to withstand such beautiful
agony.

-intimidation often hides behind control

I will always be too much to people who do not
have enough strength to hold me. I do not deal
with half measures, because you cannot hold me
with anything less than two hands, all in. I am
not too loud, or too much, I am confident and
powerful. Too powerful to acknowledge anyone
who disagrees, indirect disrespect screams a
mediocrity that I couldn't comprehend. I am a
work of art, a mural that is never truly
understood, but carefully crafted and marveled
at. I refuse to apologize for inconsistent eyes that
can't recognize my views and hands that can't
handle my handles. It has never been that i am
too much, but yet, that they are too little.

-can you take a hit?

When life hits you so hard, it knocks your teeth out, and fills your mouth with blood, what else can you do besides fall back into the earth and let the dirt keep you, as you always knew it would?

-descendent of Medusa

5

I never could stand my own reflection, but I
would let your eyes turn me to stone, just for a
moment to get lost in them.

-maturity

I know I've grown because the old me would've erupted with a flow of molten lava so hot, it would've destroyed everything until you were nothing more than blazed bone fragments and pain.

-a heart made from the space,
distant and lonely

The only savior I've ever had from my own
thoughts was a tear-stained paper, and a pen
made from stardust.

-the Milky Way, confined

You don't even know what an artist I am with words, because the galaxies in your eyes always made me forget how to align them.

-sacrifice, at the cost of me

At one time, I swear that you put the stars in the sky. I would've bet my life that you made the earth rotate, the stability in a world that never seemed so. I put you on a shelf so high, that the tallest skyscrapers couldn't even imagine to your views. It was incredible and beautiful, yet it was exhausting and all consuming. You were a light so bright that my eyes never adjusted, and when you were gone, my eyes closed permanently, desperate to recreate your daze. You were an unmatched flame, and I was the moth willing to burn inside you.

-feelings I will never untangle

Hurt looks like hate from a distance. Pain looks like rage from afar. The two feelings have always been similar in my heart, always getting lost in translation.

-you wanted space, but I had
galaxies at my disposal

You were a moment of solace from the restless
black hole in my mind. A radiant star that was
eventually too tired of fighting my gravity, for
the heat of my sun, leaving me to wither in my
own flames. Little did you know, I bewitched
the blaze and danced in the ashes.

-a wormhole inside of me

When I pass on, and my body becomes one with the earth again, don't spend your time trying to find me in beautiful places. Don't look for me in the fields of flowers, or in the comfort of a sunset. Look for me in the infinite emptiness of space, and the deepest trenches in the ocean. Look for things that are endless and never understood. I am not the golden rays that warms everything in its gaze, I am the darkness inside of a black hole, blinding with one look. I am the space that holds the world's greatest mysteries and darkest forms of life. Only understandable when you find yourself one with the void.

-bitterly burned from the heart

My anger is like a natural disaster. It takes a devastating form, and destroys anyone in its path. It is uncaring and visceral, the hottest burning forest fire, disintegrating everything in sight. There is no worldly thing alike, as it is a cosmic fury that this space time has never before seen. The damage it leaves in its wake is disastrous, infectious. It seeps inside your soul, and leaves charred ash in your veins.

-i've lived in these flames my entire life

I've spent my entire life scratching away at the flesh I hated, desperate to change it. I couldn't see a life where I wanted anything less than to rip myself to shreds and come anew like a phoenix from the ashes. People aren't phoenixes' though, we do not come back from withstanding the flames. Instead, our skin melts and falls off the bones that once kept us so stable. Instead, here I lay, here I rot, with the claw marks still left scored in my bones.

-lifelong aftermath of watching death

The cold has always made me feel more at home than any place ever could. The first time I found home in the brutalizing polar, it was so glacial that my fingertips lost feeling, turning blue, and I wondered if that's how he felt. I wondered if he felt the frost spread through his body until it made a home inside of him and kept him there forever. I swore that when I gave in, the cold would take me too. So, when I finally did let the ice break apart every nerve in my body until I felt comfort in the cold, I expected nothing short of taking my last breath. Instead, the cold built a house, built a life, and became the only place where you can find the little girl who I once was. She is trapped inside that house, freezing to death in the tundra that I built to protect her.

-divine violence

She tastes like gold. The kind of gold that's so
pure, you can't indulge for anything less than
war. And oh god, is it war.

-betrayal from the inside

When it's kill or be killed, my empathy would
sacrifice me for any sad story.

-mimic

I try to find myself in everyone around me.
Asking them who I am, only to find the version
of me that's never truly existed. A version of me
that I've only ever seen in other peoples cracked
mirrors. If they knew the true me, they wouldn't
be able to stomach it, for it would show them
their own wretched and empty reflection.

-in a galaxy far, far away

He was divine intervention, and I, divine darkness. When two storms of outer- force join together, I swear it looks like a supernova.

-gang violence is a vicious cycle

My empathetic heart bleeds for my enemies. People who've tried to kill me, I hurt thinking about what brought them there. I ache thinking about the life and choices they romanticize, knowing it is a vow, not until death will they part.

-pancakes, bacon, and love on a Sunday morning in March

On days like this, the sun shines exclusively for him, existing only to poke through the kitchen curtains and act as a spotlight on his eyes, eyes that have always found me in a crowded room. Then, when he finally cracks at the ribs, and the most beautifully orchestrated laugh breaks the sound barriers in the air, i swear, it would make the biggest cynic turn pink in the cheeks.